momentum

Amy Haddlesey

BookLeaf
Publishing

India | USA | UK

Presentation by *BookLeaf Publishing*

Web: www.bookleafpub.com

E-mail: info@bookleafpub.com

ISBN: 9789357619493

First edition 2023

Now / then

I'm a time traveler
Years have gone by
And I can still put myself
in those old shoes
in those old feelings

I can pull on the guilt
The shame
The resentment
Like an old sweater
or old skin

And be transported back to you, yelling
Angry at your little girl
Terrified she'd outgrown you

It haunts me still
That I've had to reconcile
Love and anger
Love and fear

I had to learn how to make myself small
To still fit
But eventually the seams stretch
The threads fray

And it makes more sense to hurt you
Than make myself stay

My thousand cuts

I had a dream about a weird reality
There were people out to kill me,
throwing knives from every angle
that only I could see

Constantly looking
fearful of where the malice would come from
next
Every corner was a trial,
every stranger was a judge

Do you give in because the end's inevitable
or let yourself believe it isn't?
People were confused and didn't understand
as they saw me desperately try to protect
myself
from this unseen threat.

I struggled and pushed against
some invisible man as his knife drew near.
In the knife's reflection I saw my own face,
contorted in aggression and fear

I don't even remember if my adversary had a
face
it didn't seem important
No one came to help me and I thought
maybe this reality isn't so strange
after all

My fight left me
I gave in
I saw my face go slack as his knife turned to
water,
and suddenly everyone could see it
wash over my throat.

Hurt / hurting

When I was young you traced my skin on the
same locations
Where your own scars were housed
Marvelling at my unblemished skin
My love for the world and ability to live in it

Then as I got older still
The expression on your face,
as you traced
Went from awe
To trepidation

Your hand shook and you didn't trust yourself
To leave me unmarked
- I still trusted you then too

I could see beyond your lashings
To the man that loved me and was hurting
I could shoulder the hardships of being loved by
you
I could see your harsh words but choose the
love underneath

Then I got older still

Bit by bit
A little less willing to sign up for hurt

The injuries you laid against me
Started to break the skin
You were broken
So you broke me too
As if your jagged edge
Sliced a mirror image of your own scars into me

They healed slower and slower
Their slices grew harder to repair
Harder to ignore
When they did heal I could see the ugly scars
they left behind

The older ones I long thought healed
Started to ache - their pain began anew
As I traced these scars on my skin
I wondered how they could ever be tokens of
love
How I withstood so much, for so long

I grew to understand
That these would be your legacy to me
One I would carry with me
No matter how healed

A lesson only learned in repetition
Love shouldn't hurt this much

Go / stay

I'd always thought you must have gotten it so
wrong

You misunderstood
But maybe not
Maybe I had

I thought I wanted you
to make an effort
Work for your spot in my life

But maybe I wanted you
to give up your seat
Then I just couldn't stop staring at the empty
chair

Hungry

You can't stop time
You can't skip the bad parts
But you can give them less power

Give more power,
More time,
More attention

To your favourite parts
Your favourite textures
To joy

To the moments you love yourself
Dwell in them
Sink into them
Take a bite

Sense / feel

I have a short attention span
Same with my feelings
- most of the time

Others I get stuck in, for days
Quicksand
Pulled under
The undertow

I hardly know which way is up
I've been falling for so long
I've lost my sense
Too far down the rabbit hole

Weeping isn't the word
The tears slide silently out
It's like looking at my life
Through a looking glass

It's hard to know what's real
When you make sense
Of the world around you
Through your emotions

But most of the time
emotions don't make sense
They make you

Goddess reflected

I was looking at myself in the mirror
When the late afternoon light caught my hair
On fire
It was more lustrous than I was used to
More fiery than I felt

For a moment it felt wonderful
To be someone else
With sparks in her veins
And an angel's touch in her hair

Something the devil would covet
But could never touch
Was it a burden or a blessing
To be untouchable

Or was it worse
To be touched
And feel nothing at all

There's a specific ache
To be touched while thinking of someone else
That turns your moans to ash in your mouth

This fiery goddess looking back at me
In the mirror
Red lips
A challenge in her eyes
Would never understand

What it felt like
To be touched
To allow herself to be touched
And feel nothing
Nothing at all

Glitter

I can feel it sucking
everything in - everything good

I'm not afraid of it
This thing that eats up the light
But I'm aware that for the next little while
my feelings can't be trusted

That my view of the world might be
a little skewed
That something else is running the show

I can't wait
For the world to glitter again

Fear me

Don't look at me like that
Don't use that voice with me
I recognize the source of both -
Pity

And it kills me you'd use that
weapon against me
Because it is a weapon

It makes me feel small and helpless
I've choked on my insecurities
And still kept my head held high

Don't comfort me,
I need none.

Cut / open

Art brings existing pieces into
a new arrangement
Yet we call it creation,
As if it's born from nothing.

Or not nothing - but the intangible
Born from the things about you,
no one could ever touch
Or hold.

Something used to the dark
Thrust into the lime,
Bleary-eyed and blinking,
I hope it can stand.

Chaos / white noise

Lately it can feel like I'm addicted
to filling my head,
rather than letting it empty.
I consume, consume, consume

But what does it matter if I don't reflect?
If I don't digest?
If I don't take a stance?

I want to consume for a purpose
for a pursuit
I want to be seeking out data to understand
a truth worth knowing

A truth about me
Or others
Or the world I woke up in

I want to be able to tell the difference
between my own choices and a world
so interdependent
That where I've found myself
Tends to just be wherever the river's carried me

The more I fill my head
The quieter my own voice becomes

Have you ever woken up
in the middle of the night,
and the TV is still playing?

Living / in your grave

We can wake up,
go through the motions,
get comfy, and settle in
to our fine grooves.

Then not notice the dirt rising up around us,
as we're buried alive.
Not notice until we're choking on it,
running out of air,
As the hourglass fills.

Smothered by our complacency and stagnation
Maybe there are moments that shake you
Urge you to snap out of it -
But maybe there aren't.

Maybe you can't wait
for the bus to hit you
Or someone beautiful to break your heart

Maybe those moments are so fleeting
you can shrug them off
Remove them from your mind
And settle back into your rut, your grave

Stop waiting for your shake-up
Stop looking for the hero in your story
Wake up
Sit up
Spit out the dirt
And get out

Dark / moon

I've painted wings on my back
I've seen horns in my reflection

Sometimes it feels good to blame
someone else
The devil's in you
Your demons have the wheel

It feels even better though
To be bad
To be accused a witch
And burn the village to the ground

To be wicked
And unexpected
To be full of dark magic
Dancing in a graveyard
Beneath the full moon

Womanhood as madness
Darkness as comfort
Step off the pedestal
And come play in the night

Self preservation is murder

Am I thankful?
Does it make me more interesting?
My writing better?

Or am I just another sad little girl
hooked on her own drama
Too self-involved to see
that making you my villain
makes it easier

Easier to abandon you
to the darkness that took you
bit by bit
And left an angry stranger
in your place

Did I let you drown
so you wouldn't take me with you?
(Or did I find the shore
and push your head under?)

Haunted / forgotten

Certain days bear our scars
They are (forever) marked
They reverberate in an empty theatre
And make us hollow
The echoes get faint
The candle goes out
And suddenly you're standing alone in the dark

Unconditional / love

Have you ever felt fear in the silence on the
phone?
Where each passing second is accompanied by
something inside of you
constricting a little more
Where you feel nothing of you exists beyond
the sound of your breath
Anxious and short

I waited and waited, steeling myself for your
rage
It never came - this time
But I felt in that silence echoes of before

They made me flinch when you said easily
That's okay, I understand
It's as if I heard what you said but my body
remembered differently
Remembering, my chest tightened and these
echoes opened old wounds
Wounds that did not ache in certain weather,
but in certain conversations I had
Others who relied on me just as much

and whose love pressed down on me just as
hard

They too caused these scars to burn and hurt all
over again
How anyone could say love is unconditional I'm
not sure
I've heard its conditions yelled at me
I've seen the consequences of not meeting its
terms

The end of the call came and you said I love
you, talk to you soon
And I wondered if you said it so I would hear it
So I know I'm loved and cherished
Or if it's so I'll say it back
And sign for another term

A reassurance you need to ensure you can
control me
There's a beat of silence
Enough hesitation to notice,
little enough to forget once I say I love you too
(Unconditionally)
And I suppose after all this, it must be true

Fighting / a pacifist

Sometimes I feel like we're in a standoff
Both mad and hurt by the other for the same
things
Neither willing to put down our guns

But then I remember how many times I stood in
front of you
And let you shoot me
Each blow because you loved me too much
Or I didn't call enough
Each blow for the reasons I'm lacking

It took me a while to realize
You broke the rules
You fired at someone who wouldn't fire back
Who wouldn't walk away
Then wondered where your little girl went

Closed off / healing

I think what I felt today
Was myself hit a barrier / a limit
Where to keep going
Was to de-value myself

To tell myself
You do not deserve peace
You are not safe here
You will not be treated as delicately as others
Your shortcomings will not be met with
tenderness

But that's not the world I want to build around
myself
I want a world where when your cup empties
You can close the door
I want my world to be home

Where you are forgiven
Where you are not broken or behind
Where you are sacred and iridescent
I feel my leaves close around me
And fold in my petals
I close the door

Laughter / silence

It's not uncommon
For me
To hear laughter in another room
And wonder
If laughter is sweeter when I'm not around

If life goes so unceasingly on
That absences are not truly felt
Until you realize someone's laughter
Will never again mix with your own

Alternate / reality

I felt like a slight rush of air
Would break me
So I went for a run in high winds

I refuse to believe I'm so small
That I can trust the limits I've thought for myself

My grandest dreams
And harshest thoughts
Can barely co-exist

So if I had to look between them
And shoot the clone
The one not truly of this world
I'd choose the one
screaming at me
You'll never be enough

Open / wounds

My weakness is stories
My weakness is magic
My weakness is belief

What my weaknesses are
Are the cracks and weak spots in the wall I've
built
The facade that keeps me from feeling exposed
and vulnerable
But keeps me from feeling

My weaknesses sneak in
And sneak under
They not only reach me
They enter me and leave openings in their wake
That I thought before were wounds

But realize now
Are doorways